Volcanoes

Michele Ingber Drohan

The Rosen Publishing Group's
PowerKids Press™
New York

To Betsy, for giving me infinite encouragement and inspiration.

Published in 1999 by The Rosen Publishing Group, Inc.
29 East 21st Street, New York, NY 10010

First Edition

Book Design: Danielle Primiceri

Photo Credits and Photo Illustrations: Cover © Warren Faidley/International Stock; p. 5 by Danielle Primiceri; pp. 6, 13 © Warren Faidley/International Stock; p. 9 © Greg Johnston; p. 10 © Ron Behrmann/International Stock; p. 14 © Telegraph Colour Library/FPG International; p. 17 © Ron Sanford/International Stock; p. 18 © Buddy Mays/International Stock; p. 21 © Kenfre, Inc./International Stock; p. 22 © Wilson North/International Stock.

Drohan, Michele Ingber.
    Volcanoes / Michele Ingber Drohan.
        p.   cm.— (Natural disasters)
    Includes index.
    Summary: Explains the different types of volcanoes, where they are located, what causes them to erupt, and how people protect themselves from an eruption.
    ISBN 0-8239-5284-3
    1. Volcanoes—Juvenile literature. [1. Volcanoes.]   I. Title. II. Series: Drohan, Michele Ingber. Natural disasters.
QE521.3.D76 1998
551.21—dc21
                                                                97-43119
                                                                    CIP
                                                                    AC

Manufactured in the United States of America

Contents

Earth's Layers

Earth is made of three layers of rock. The top layer is called the crust. The crust is solid rock and covers the whole surface of Earth. We live on the crust. The middle layer is called the **mantle** (MAN-tul). The mantle is solid rock filled with pockets of liquid rock, called **magma** (MAG-muh). The center of Earth is called the core. The core is part magma and part solid rock. The closer you get to Earth's core, the hotter it gets. The distance from Earth's crust to the center of the core is about 4,000 miles.

Compared to the mantle and the core, Earth's crust is very thin. ▶

CRUST

MANTLE

CORE

What Is a Volcano?

The crust of Earth is broken into many pieces called **plates** (PLAYTS). The plates are always moving. But you don't feel it because they move very slowly—only about two inches every year. A volcano forms when there is a crack in Earth's crust either between plates or in the middle of them. This can happen in two ways. One way is when the plates break apart, causing a **rift zone** (RIFT ZOHN). Another way is when they bump into each other and one plate forces the other one down into the mantle, forming a **subduction zone** (sub-DUK-shun ZOHN). When the cracks in these zones let magma through the crust, it's called a **volcanic eruption** (vol-KA-nik ee-RUP-shun). When magma reaches the surface of Earth, it's called **lava** (LAH-vuh).

▶ When lava flows out it is very, very hot. It will melt or burn almost everything that gets in its way.

Types of Volcanoes

Many people think that volcanoes always look like mountains. But there are four kinds of volcanoes, all with different shapes. Sometimes volcanoes do look like mountains. These form when magma comes out of Earth's crust and cools into hard rock. Over time this rock builds up into the shape of a mountain. Mount St. Helens in Washington State, Mount Fuji in Japan, and Mount Vesuvius in Italy were all made this way. They are called **stratovolcanoes** (STRA-toh-vol-CAY-noz). The three other types of volcanoes are called shield, cinder-cone, and dome volcanoes. They get their names because of their shapes.

This is Volcan de San Miguel, a stratovolcano in El Salvador. ▶

Where Are Volcanoes Found?

Volcanoes are found all over the world. Many are located in the countries around the Pacific Ocean. Scientists call this the Ring of Fire. All of the volcanoes in this area are from subduction zones. Most of these volcanoes are **dormant** (DOR-ment). This means they haven't erupted in a long time.

The Mid-Atlantic Rift Zone is found in the middle of the Atlantic Ocean. It has the most active volcanoes in the world. This means they erupt a lot. But you can't see them because they are under the ocean!

▼ *This is Mount Fuji in Japan. It is one of the volcanoes in the Ring of Fire.*

Hot Spots

Volcanoes usually form where two plates meet. But sometimes a volcano can form right in the middle of a plate. This is called a hot spot. Scientists don't know why this happens. But they do know how it happens. A hot spot is where magma melts right through the plate. This forms a volcano. Scientists believe that this is how volcanoes on Hawaii were made. Mauna Loa is the largest of many volcanoes on Hawaii. It is 70 miles long and 30,000 feet high.

Kilauea is one of Hawaii's most famous and active volcanoes. ▼

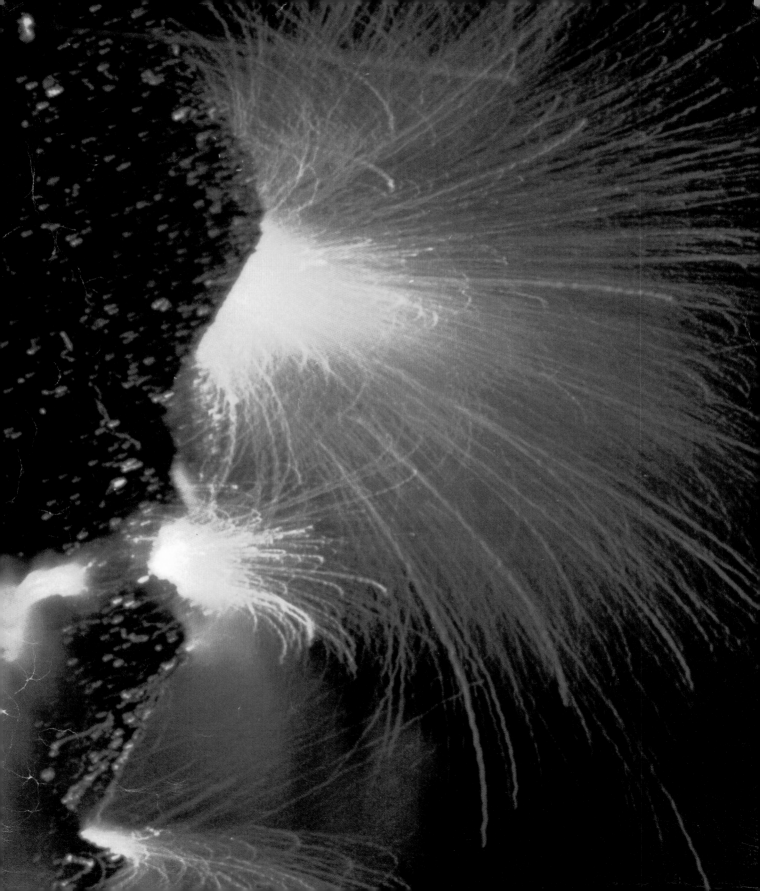

Eruption!

Volcanoes erupt in different ways. In a Hawaiian-type eruption, lava flows out freely, like hot fudge on ice cream. A **phreatic** (free-AH-tik) eruption is when steam, created by water touching the magma inside a volcano, is released. It looks like steam from a boiling kettle. Phreatic eruptions usually occur under the ocean.

Other kinds of eruptions happen on land. One is called a **Plinian** (PLIH-nee-an) eruption. It looks like a big mushroom cloud. The most violent kind of eruption is called a **Strombolian** (strom-BOH-lee-in) eruption. When this happens, thick lava blocks gases from getting out of the top of the volcano. When enough gas builds up, it shoots the hot rock and lava high into the air.

▶ *A Strombolian eruption, such as this one, looks like fireworks shooting out of a volcano.*

Rescue

A volcano erupting near a town or city is very dangerous. Gases damage the air. Clouds of hot ash can move as fast as 60 miles per hour. The first thing to do if there is an eruption is to get to a safe place. Hot, flowing lava will destroy everything in its path. Rescuers try to stop the flow of lava to save people's homes. They spray the lava with water from fire hoses to cool it. When lava cools, it slows down and then stops. But it can take a long time to stop a lava flow. Sometimes a volcano erupts for many months, even years. A volcano on an island in the Caribbean Sea called Soufriere Hills has been erupting since 1995. Thousands of people have been forced to leave the island.

In Hawaii, this lava flow from Kilauea covered 1/4 mile of road in one day! ▶

Can You Predict a Volcanic Eruption?

Knowing when a volcano is going to erupt can save lives. **Volcanologists** (VOL-kuh-NOL-uh-jists) are people who study volcanoes. They use special instruments to try to **predict** (pre-DIKT) when a volcano will erupt. One instrument is called a **seismometer** (syz-MAH-meh-ter). It is used to measure movement in the ground. When magma pushes through a crack in Earth's crust the ground near the volcano shifts. So if the seismometer says that the ground is moving a lot, the volcanologist knows that the volcano may erupt at any time. But even with these instruments, scientists can't be exactly sure when a volcano will erupt. But they still try. The more exact they can be, the more people they can save.

▶ *Sometimes volcanoes give a lot of warning before they erupt. Other times they give no warning at all.*

Mount St. Helens

In 1978 volcanologists predicted that Mount St. Helens would erupt some time in the next ten years. They were right. Mount St. Helens erupted in 1980. Many people were saved because they were told the volcano would erupt. They left before it happened. But 57 people who did not leave were killed by the blast. Homes, highways, and forests were destroyed. It was the worst eruption in the history of the United States. In 1982 the area became the Mount St. Helens National Volcanic Monument. Many people visit it every year to learn about volcanoes.

When Mount St. Helens erupted, ash and rock did not just come out the top. In fact, the whole north side of the mountain exploded! ▼

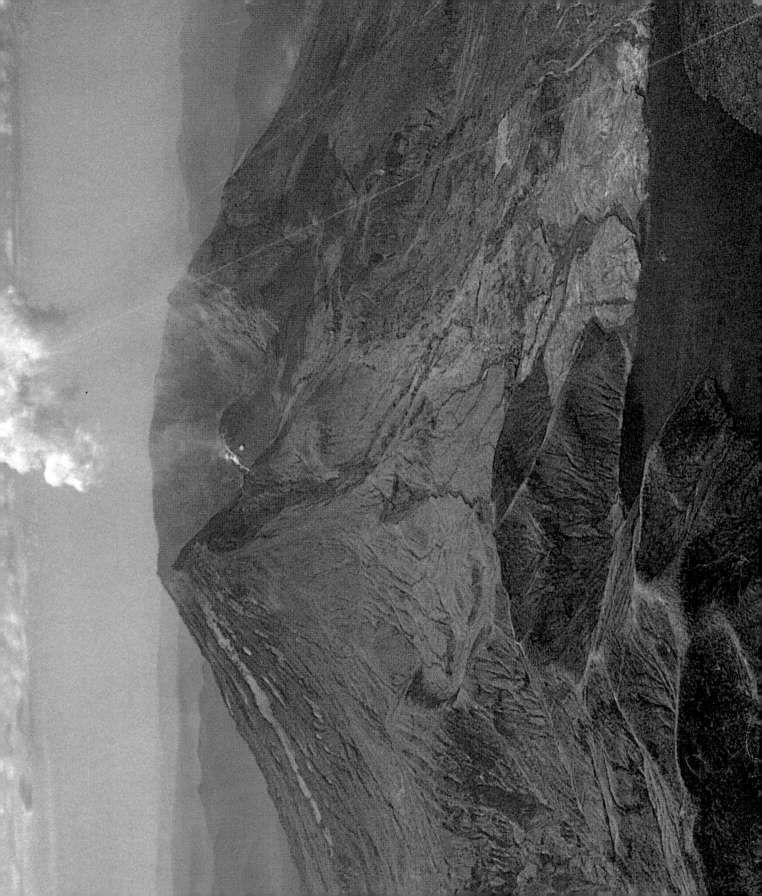

Nature's Course

Even though volcanoes are dangerous, they give Earth many good things too. The heat inside a volcano can be used to make electricity. Lava rock is used to make new roads. Diamonds and metals such as copper and tin are usually found near volcanoes. The ash from volcanoes is good for Earth's soil. The ash makes the soil rich. Rich soil is good for growing plants and food. Soon after a volcanic eruption, life returns and grows again.

Web Sites:

You can learn more about volcanoes at these Web sites:

http://www.fema.gov/kids/

http://volcano.und.nodak.edu/vw.html

Glossary

dormant (DOR-ment) When something is sleeping, such as a volcano that hasn't erupted in a very long time.

lava (LAH-vuh) What magma is called when it reaches the surface of Earth.

magma (MAG-muh) The hot, liquid rock inside the mantle.

mantle (MAN-tul) The middle layer of Earth. It is made of solid rock with pockets of magma.

phreatic (free-AH-tik) A type of eruption where steam is created by water hitting magma.

plates (PLAYTS) The moving pieces of Earth's crust.

Plinian (PLIH-nee-an) A type of eruption that creates a huge mushroom cloud.

predict (pre-DIKT) To know something is going to happen before it happens.

rift zone (RIFT ZOHN) When two plates break apart and make a crack in Earth's crust.

seismometer (syz-MAH-meh-ter) An instrument used to measure movement in Earth.

stratovolcano (STRA-toh-vol-CAY-noh) A type of volcano that looks like a mountain.

Strombolian (strom-BOH-lee-in) A violent volcanic eruption where lava and rocks are shot high into the air.

subduction zone (sub-DUK-shun ZOHN) When two plates hit, one forces the other into the mantle, and a crack is formed.

volcanic eruption (volKA-nik ee-RUP-shun) When magma comes through a crack in Earth's crust.

volcanologist (VOl-kuh-NOL-uh-jist) A person who studies volcanoes.

Index

On your marks
Get set

Cirque du Soleil
at Bellagio

Photographs by Véronique Vial

Introduction by Franco Dragone

Poems by Kerry Fleming

pH powerHouse Books, nyc

Water. We began with an idea, a transparent idea, an idea breathtaking in its overarching simplicity: to return to the dawn of time, to the primordial element in order to recount the human experience. Naively, like explorers, we embarked on a conquest without fully realizing our audacity, or the dangers of this endeavor.

Water. Without measuring the stakes, we launched a challenge. We attempted to master an element that throughout history has defied human control. Inexorably, water has always slipped through the fingers of mankind.

We began building a machine to harness the water, to bend it to our will.

Inevitably, though, the theatrical machine began to overwhelm us. The more we tried to control the element of water, the more we risked denying its beauty, its grandeur. It became a battle between the man-made machine and nature.

Lost somewhere in the middle, human frailty.

I became the guardian of the human element, that fragile poetry of human experience revealed by small gestures, almost insignificant moments. In the epic battle of domination that evolved onstage between nature and the machine, I sided with the characters to help express their fears, their wonderment, their life-and-death struggle to understand. They became my children, my fathers and mothers, my enemies, my brothers. Through them I sought to weave the fabric of human experience.

Water. "O." A human tale, I hope, somewhere between nature and the machine.

—Franco Dragone
Writer and Director, "O" Cirque du Soleil

O behold
a story told
of grace
and beauty

Hand in hand
we set out
to discover
the riches
of the universe
are all within

O love of mine
from the depths of imagination
still dripping with desire
where will you lead me today?

O the wind of change doth blow
in which direction who can know
I dare not ask I turn and go
I'll find out when I get there

O the world's a stage
they say
upon which mortals
strut and play
until the final hour of day
until the curtain calls

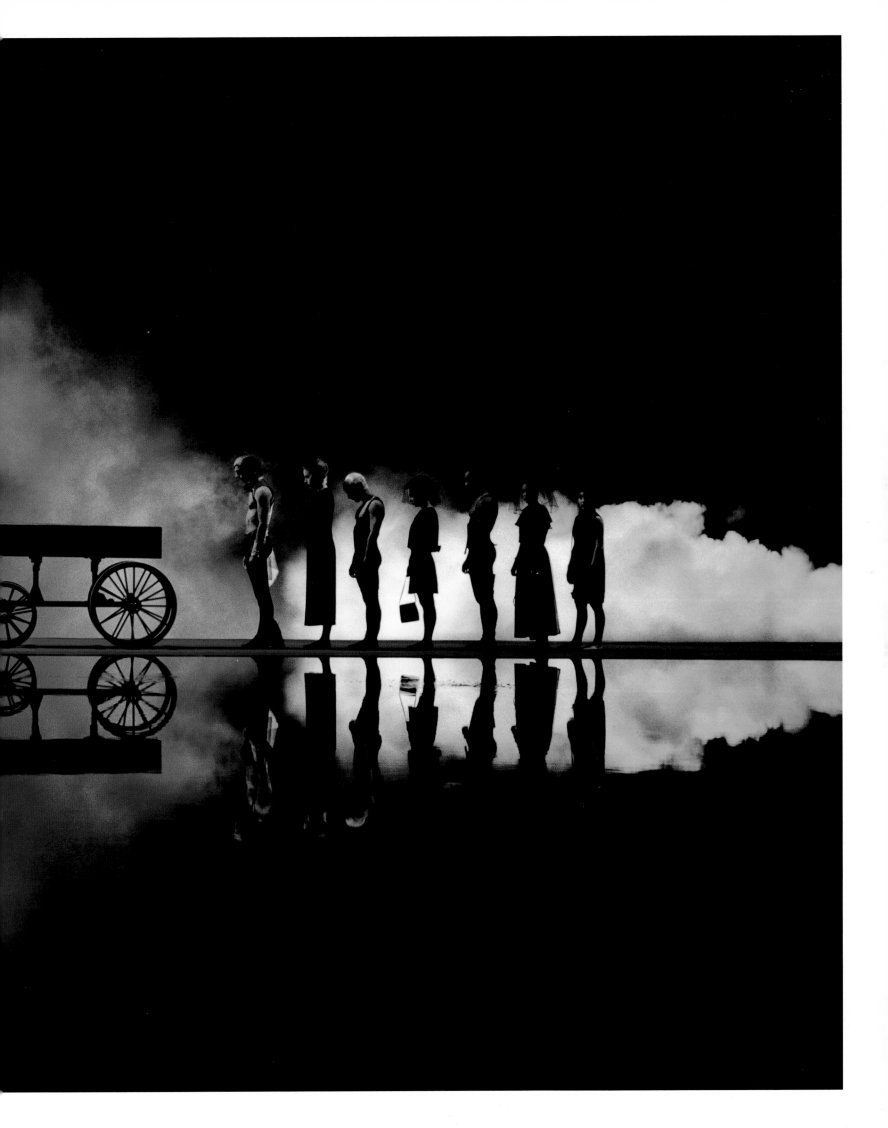

So begins the show
shrouds and footsteps
to and fro
exchanging places
quid pro quo

A time will come
for everyone
a fleeting moment
but O what fun

Free at last
of this mortal coil
a knot untied
the end of toil
the end of struggle
an answered plea
a bell tolls joyously
for thee

Suspended
between light and dark
we leave our mark
on life the spark
that burns so brightly
for an instant
and then just fades away

Terra firma
home again
forget the journey
deny the pain
forget discovery
but then again
if you remain
you'll surely go insane

Don't give up
you must escape
grab hold and pull
it's not too late
You've one last chance
to swim and dance
I beg you please don't wait

O circle, o the cycle
ô la vie, an ode to thee
O water of life
please carry me
O

Dance be nimble
dance be quick
the sky above
the sea so thick
it beckons us to slip inside
but be careful
it's a trick

Synchronicity
rising tide
the waves await
come for a ride
dive right in
they'll carry you
safely to my side

A heart can be stolen
as any thief should know
but with a little sleight of hand
you can even steal the show

Travel far and wide my friend
journey to the very end
you think you've found it all
and then
you finally find yourself

My back bears all
yet I stand tall
my legs are strong
I will not fall
I'm neither man nor beast to call
don't shoulder me with burden

A circle or a sphere
a symbol of our fear
perhaps the home
   of beings unknown
the start of a new year

Tic tac O
in the game of life go slow
one false move
Your chance to prove
there can be no tomorrow

Noble beast
winged messenger of death
do not alight
I pray thee
grant me one more night

Ophelia, dear
obey your heart
drown your sorrow
in the name of art
I love you so
but we must part
the end is growing near

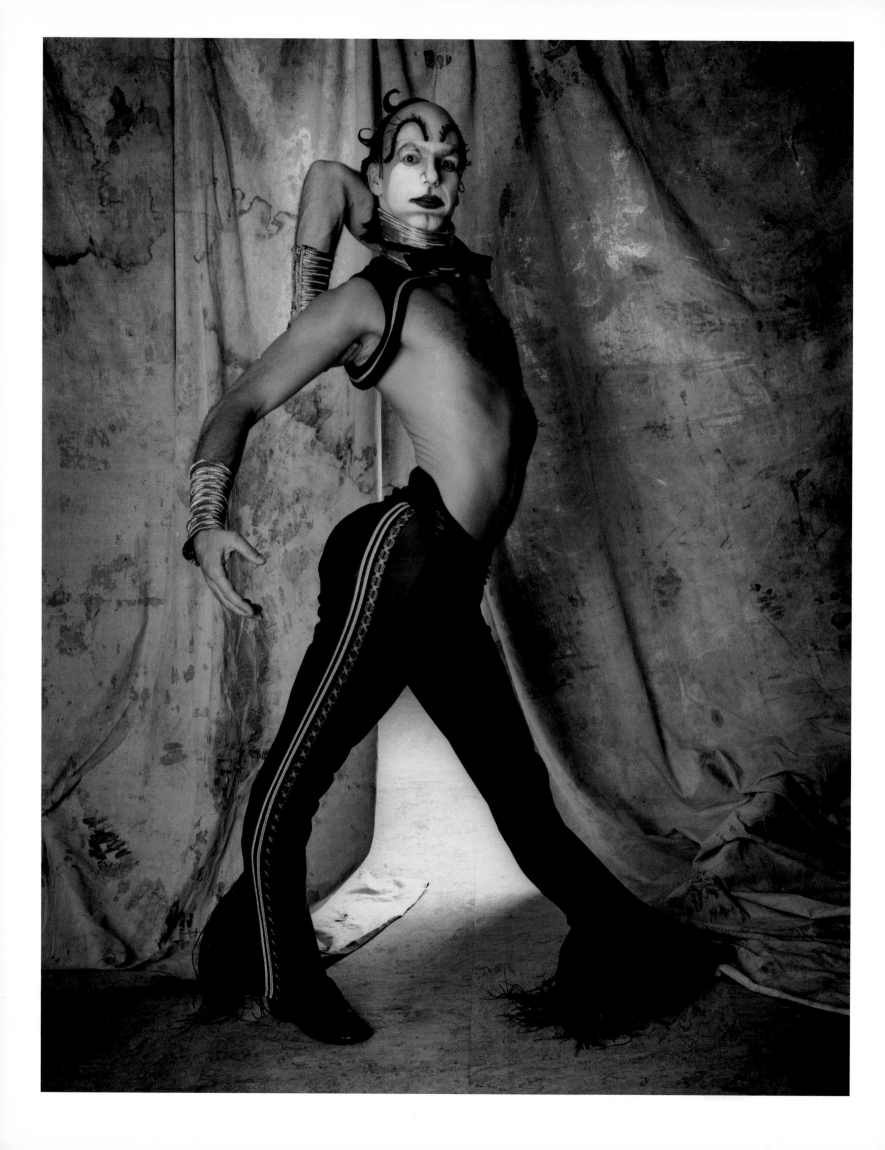

Pas de deux for you
the dance of death
adieu
the closing act
came much too soon
but hey
that's entertainment

acknowledgements

Thank you to all my friends
at
Cirque du Soleil
and
to Guy Laliberté

who supported my vision since my
beginning!

Nage

Just as water is essential to all life, the swimmers' graceful presence, during the acts and transitional segues, is central to "O." At the heart of the production, the swimmers provide the necessary link between the elements of fire, earth, air, and water. Choreographed by Debra Brown and Olympic gold medalist Sylvie Fréchette, the synchronized swimming team is made up of 16 world-class swimmers.

Performers: Tyna Agostinelli, Benoît Beaufils, Stéphanie Bissonnette, Johanne Clerk, Sylvie Dumaine, Paula Holmwood, Kari Kreitzer, Becky Lancer, Stéphane Miermont, Isabelle Proulx-St-Cyr, Chantal Sauvageau, Katy Savoie, Katia Séréno, Jill Smith, Isabelle Thomas; *Coach*: Sylvie Fréchette; *Choreography*: Debra Brown and Sylvie Fréchette; *Underwater Consultant*: Jacky Beffroi

(*Nage* = Synchronized Swimming)

Duo Trapèze

Two aerialists perform their dance in the air, sharing a single trapeze designed to co-exist with the water and machinery of the Bellagio Theatre. To create this visually stunning mirror image, the act was choreographed suspended from the massive overhead carousel. Their breath-taking maneuvers and feet-to-feet catches emulate the beauty of harmony and complete trust.

Performers: Karyne Steben and Sarah Steben

Solo Trapèze

Performers: Nataliya Grybova; *Coaches*: André Vallerand, Andre Simard, Philippe Chartrand; *Choreography Consultant*: Pavel Brun

Barge

With amazing strength and fearlessness, this team of talented acrobats performs atop a floating raft in the Barge act. The core group is comprised of eight women who are world-champion sports acrobats. Their act combines innovative gymnastic performances with banquine, a traditional circus act, and the balletic prowess of adagio. Blending these skills with water completes this high-energy act, which also includes synchronized swimmers and Olympic divers.

Performers: Stephen Bland, Irina Borbounevitch, Anastassia Dobrynina, Yuliya Eremina, Oleg Fedossov, Colin Follenweider, Nadejda Koudriavtseva, Siarhei Kudrevich, John Maxson, Tatyana Mironovich, Tatiana Nikitenko, Vadim Pavlov, Tomasz Rossa, Viktor Rybouchkine, Marina Shabelnaya, Elena Solodovnikova, Irina Syrova, Anna Zarianova; *Coach*: Tom Otjes; *Choreography*: Debra Brown

Bateau

Charting the course of life and the pursuit of dreams, this steel-frame ship floats above the water and provides the platform for this truly unique display of acrobatic timing and strength. At the foundation of the Bateau (French for boat) is the traditional circus discipline of the aerial cradle act, which is incorporated with gymnastics parallel bars for the very first time. This dynamic presentation, performed without safety lines or nets, brings the delicate balance of air and water to life. The ten performers, including three women, are made up of flyers and catchers.

Performers: Didier Antoine, Stephen Bland, Philippe Chartrand, Olivier Lefebure, Daniel Headecker, Véronique Jean, Amélie Major, Benoit Potvin, Guillermo Reyes, Vincent Schonbrodt, Lisa Simes, Craig Paul Smith, Kent Thomson; *Coaches*: Didier Antoine, Amélie Major, Tom Otjes, Andre Simard; *Choreography*: Debra Brown; *Aerial Design*: Andre Simard, Jaque Paquin

Feu

The rage of fire and the purification of water are blended into one—and then displayed throughout the "O" theatre in this brilliantly visual act. Incorporating ancient folklore and martial arts, this act invokes rituals from countries around the world including Hawaii, Samoa, New Zealand, and Australia. The fire act was conceptualized and transformed by four artists with different professional backgrounds, from performance companies to street theatre.

Performers: Michael Brown, Fua'au "Junior" Faitau, Tuione Lisiate Tovo, Ray Wold

(*Feu* = Fire)

Russian Swing

Pleasure, envy, passion, and temptation are everywhere during the honeymoon celebration. Drawing on inspiration from the many wedding chapels throughout Las Vegas, the church bell atop the largest swing calls all to join the party…life, love, and death. The cast includes expert divers who use three sets of Russian Swings. The swinging movement of the swing creates a varied trajectory of flight, making it a challenge even for a seasoned diver. Moving from the initial point at ground level to the highest point at thirty-two feet creates a momentary weightlessness, followed by tremendous acceleration back down to the water.

Performers: Didier Antoine, Terry Bartlett, Stephen Bland, Irina Borbounevitch, Philippe Chartrand, Anastassia Dobrynina, Yuliya Eremina, Oleg Fedossov, Daniel Headecker, Véronique Jean, Colin Follenweider, Sairhei Kudrevich, Mathieu LaPlante, Amélie Major,

John Maxson, Tatyana Mironovich, Tatiana Nikitenko, Vadim Pavlov, Benoit Potvin, Tomasz Rossa, Viktor Rybouchkine, Elena Solodovnikova, Kent Thomson, Anna Zarianova; *Coach:* André Vallerand; *Choreography:* Debra Brown; *Aerial Design:* Jaque Paquin

Cadre

Trying to maintain balance in a stormy universe, the zebras constantly realign themselves, hanging on until the very end. Resembling a playground jungle gym, this giant aerial frame was created by Cirque du Soleil specialists to facilitate choreography and gymnastics in the aerial space between the sky and the water. Featuring many performers from the Bateau act, the entire number takes place suspended in mid-air.

Performers: Terry Bartlett, Benoît Beaufils, Olivier Lefebure, Daniel Headecker, Véronique Jean, Kari Kreitzer, Amélie Major, Guillermo Reyes, Vincent Schonbrodt, Lisa Simes, Craig Paul Smith, Kent Thomson; *Coaches:* André Vallerand, Amélie Major; *Choreography:* Debra Brown; *Aerial Design:* Jaque Paquin

High Dive

A group of four world-class high divers leap sixty feet from the grid level to a small, exposed section of the pool. The dive team is made up of experienced cliff and exhibition divers. The crowd is astonished when a seemingly innocent spectator chosen from the audience takes the plunge.

Performers: Stephen Bland, Colin Follenweider, John Maxson, Tomasz Rossa, Viktor Rybouchkine, Kent Thompson; *Coach:* André Vallerand

Trapèze Washington

The Trapèze Washington is unique because unlike the traditional rope-hung trapeze, it is built on a fixed metal frame and swings in a long pendulum-like motion. The trapeze is attached to the revolving carousel and descends from the grid at four feet per second, resulting in a heightened degree of difficulty. This segment fuses the slack wire and tightrope with the high technology of the Bellagio Theatre.

Performer: Anja Christa Wyttenbach; *Coach:* Tom Otjes

Contortion

All the way from Mongolia, these four girls have been performing since they were eight years old. Their graceful body language and lithe movements depict the balletic perfection of the female form. Their arrival from the air and their performance surrounded by water add new dimensions to this long-held circus tradition.

Performers: Dashbaljir Enkhjargal, Damba Namchinkhand, Gantumur Saraana, Tumendelger Enkhee; *Coach:* Angelique Talvot; *Choreography:* Debra Brown

Cerceaux

This act fuses dizzying aerial choreography with sublime gymnastic routines. There is a high level of movement on stage between the equipment and a group of four performers. Water acts as an element of both ambience and movement in the choreography. This traditional circus act is reinvented with the addition of water and its relationship to the sky.

Performers: Terry Bartlett, Philippe Chartrand, Anastasia Dobrynina, Colin Follenweider, Yuliya Eremina, Nataliya Grybova, Mathieu LaPlante, Tatiana Nikitenko, Benoit Potvin, Isabelle Proulx-St-Cyr, Anja Christa Wyttenbach; *Coaches:* Philippe Chartand, Samuel Journot; *Choreography:* Debra Brown

(*Cerceaux* = Aerial Hoops)

Clowns

With simple, poetic gestures the clowns convey the many complexities of life. Two unpretentious souls on a search for answers, Leonid and Valery provide light to balance with humanity's dark side. This team, originally from Russia, has been performing together since the early 1980s and was featured in Cirque du Soleil's *Alegría*.

Performers: Leonid Lekine and Valery Keft

Flying Man

Like the red comets flashing across the sky, this piece is performed by four athletes with extreme upper body strength.

Performers: Stephen Bland, Philippe Chartrand, Mathieu LaPlante, Vadim Pavlov, Benoit Potvin; *Coach:* Philippe Chartrand

Bungee Down

A sixty-foot free-fall from the grid ends with a sudden deceleration before rotating upside down into the water.

Performers: Stephen Bland, Philippe Chartrand, Siarhei Kudrevich, Mathieu LaPlante, John Maxson, Vadim Pavlov, Viktor Rybouchkine; *Aerial Design:* Jaque Paquin

Garden Swing

Inspired by an Esther Williams film, this plunge into the beautiful waters takes place during the Bateau and Russian Swing segments.

Performers: Stephen Bland, Colin Follenweider, Daniel Headecker, John Maxson, Vadim Pavlov, Viktor Rybouchkine; *Aerial Design:* Jaque Paquin

The Characters

Eugen is both our guide and the guardian of the theatre. Strong yet vulnerable, this aging theatre manager knows all and provokes us to see the dark side of "O." His ghostly orchestrations take us on a timeless journey through many different worlds as he makes his own transformation from dark to light. He embodies the cycle of life in which everything old becomes new again.

Guifà is a young Sicilian boy whose curiosity and quest for adventure transport him to a magical realm where all of his hopes, fears, and dreams can come true. He is the willing prisoner in this kaleidoscopic domain—the witness who is everywhere and everyman.

Le Travesti—wearing the clothes of a wicked woman, he coos, hisses, and murmurs—his primal cries resound throughout the theatre.

Performers:
Eugen - Eugen Brim
Guifà - Fikri Tallih
Le Travesti - Thamar Vijent
Aurora - Anja Christa Wyttenbach
Les Comètes - entire male cast
Le Voleur Masqué - Michael Brown
L'Allumé - Ray Wold
Le Waiter - Stephane Miermont
La Mariée - Cécile Ardail
Le Zèbra - Amélie Major
Le Jouer d'Orgue de Barbarie - Didier Antoine

Musicians

Haunting and lyrical, upbeat and melancholic—the music draws from the talents and backgrounds of musicians from around the world and blends them into the aquatic realm of "O." The score was composed by Benoit Jutras and is performed live by ten musicians from Canada, Brazil, Senegal, China, the United States, and Australia. The band for "O" utilizes an unusual combination of instruments: cello, Colombian guitar, African harp, bagpipes, Chinese violin, ancient woodwinds, and a variety of percussion instruments.

Performers:
Musical Director; Keyboard, Accordion - Stéphane Gariépy
Bagpipes, Medieval Woodwinds, Recorders, Vocals - Elise Guay
Drums, Percussion - François Jutras
Electric Bass, Keyboards - Rhéal Jutras
Vocals, Kora/25-string African Harp - Toumany Kouyaté
Cello, Guitar, Tiplé/Colombian Guitar, Vocals - Julie Andrea McInnes
Keyboard - Paule Morin
Lead Vocals, Flute - Roxane Potvin
Erhu/Chinese Violin - Lei Qiang
African Percussions - Kurt Rasmussen

"O" Creators

Guide - Guy Laliberté
Writer and Director - Franco Dragone
Director of Creation - Gilles Ste-Coix
Set Designer - Michel Crête
Costume Designer - Dominique Lemieux
Composer - Benoit Jutras
Choreographer - Debra Brown
Lighting Designer - Luc Lafortune
Sound Designer - Jonathan Deans
Sound Designer - François Bergeron
Artistic Director - Pavel Brun

The Technical Story

By contrasting the most technically advanced machinery in a beautiful Baroque setting, we sought to build images that evoke imagination. We used all of the tools of the theatre to tell this story and really pushed "the machine" to its limits: Deus ex Machina.

—Gilles Ste-Croix, **Director of Creation**

The Set

For me, the pool represents a pond, like a sanctuary protected by a garden. An intimate place where the sunlight shines through the forest creating translucent, stained-glass colors as it shines through the leaves. The scenery depicts the coexistence between nature and man, between the elements and the obvious technology used to bring them together.

—Michel Crête, **Set Designer**

Referred to by "O" technicians as the real "star" of the show, the overhead carousel is positioned forty-eight and a half feet above the stage on a revolutionary overhead conveyer, known as the "telepherique." The carousel can move up and downstage at three feet per second and in a circular motion at two revolutions per minute. It has four lifting winches, each with a capacity of 1,000 pounds and the ability to operate at four feet per second.

The telepherique is the theatrical equivalent to the gantry crane, with a specific difference: the highly sophisticated computerized controls perfectly synchronize all movements to create seamless mechanized and scenic pictures. It consists of six tracks each with two independent winches (for a total of twelve) to transport performers, scenery, and rigging.

One of the most striking set elements is the vegetation curtain. Made of vapor-resistant plastic, this rigid structure provides a dramatic backdrop for many acts. The vegetation curtain is made by thermoforming, a technique in which the Cirque du Soleil has developed considerable expertise. Lexan, a plastic material, is poured into an enormous mold measuring forty-five by sixty feet. Once the plastic solidifies, paint and varnish are applied.

The stage is constructed of steel and fiberglass combined with PVC and sports matting in order to make the degree of resilience as close as possible to that of the human body. The floor has thousands of small holes drilled into it to allow the water to flow through when the lifts are moving.

The Lighting

The eye, by nature is lazy. It's a bit like water down a river—it will follow the easiest path. By providing more intensity at one particular area on stage, they will want to go there naturally. In a stage such as this one, the possibilities are endless.

—Luc Lafortune, **Lighting Designer**

The lighting systems for "O" were tested and developed over a two-year period. Extensive lighting research was necessary because of the many obvious challenges the water element presented. Because water is highly reflective and actually filters different frequencies of light, experimentation with different lighting angles and colors was necessary.

One primary challenge was avoiding the introduction of electricity into the water. A pneumatic control system was implemented, along with innovative wiring and cables, to ensure the safety of those in the pool. This production boasts the world's first long-distance GFCI (ground fault circuit interruption) protected dimming system spanning 500 feet. The pool is equipped with 288 GFCI dimmers. Daily safety checks are conducted on each of the GFCI breaker switches.

A Strand system with a total of 1,695 dimmers controls the conventional lighting in the show. Dimmer controls are located in four areas throughout the theatre: in the light booth, the grid level, the pool room, and the lighting tunnel. A total of 1,815 theatrical lighting instruments are capable of delivering over four million watts of light on stage. The system is also equipped with 230 color scrollers.

The pool is equipped with 108 incandescent underwater lights with custom-designed gel covers. Additional wet/dry lighting is positioned behind the stage for back lighting. Additional pool lighting was installed in a dry lighting tunnel located beneath the stage. The tunnel has eleven underwater windows constructed of four-inch Plexiglas that are able to withstand both water pressure from the pool and intense heat from the lights in the tunnel. For ultimate flexibility, five HMI 2500s were installed in the lighting tunnel. Two 4000-watt lamps with color scrollers provide wide-spectrum studio-quality lighting in the pool. Aquatic masking is used to refract and diffuse the pool lighting.

The lighting installation for the Bellagio Theatre utilized 222,956 feet of cable—laid end to end that would be forty-two miles. Additionally, 11,761 connectors and 334,431 tie-wraps (cable fastening devices) were needed to install and secure the cables.

The overhead carousel is lit using wireless technology. These custom-made lights are operated by radio frequency. An eleven-person crew runs each show: one main console operator, one for the moving lights console, eight on follow spot, and one deck electrician.

The Costumes

All of humanity, throughout history, has had to fight to live. When civilizations get knocked down, they get on their feet and do it again. This is where I drew my inspiration for the costumes of "O."

—Dominique Lemieux, Costume Designer

The costumes of "O" are reminiscent of several periods from the fifteenth to the twentieth centuries, with a special emphasis on the Romantic period. Dominique was heavily influenced by the trends of Venice—the European meeting point between East and West—where all styles and forms come together.

Nearly sixty different costumes were developed, and up to ten variations of these concepts were created for each act. Both real and synthetic hair was used in most of the eight different wig styles. Over sixty wigs had to be hand-ventilated and tied to outfit the cast members.

Water provided countless challenges for the Cirque du Soleil costume creators. The element of water required that the costumes be made of durable materials that fit like a second skin and dry fast. To accomplish this, a silicone application was created and used on nearly forty percent of the costumes. All shoes were constructed of bull hide, which can be worn in water without shortening the life of the shoes.

Like the costumes, the use of makeup required an extensive testing process. All makeup used in the show is waterproof. A total of eighty-six different shades create an unique but unified look and the bright foundations signify the "light from within the body."

The Sound

Like every Cirque production, "O" is unique in its own way. For audio, this is the champion of uniqueness because there is no other theatre like this in the world. All of the testing and programming has to be done in the theatre with all of the elements. It is extremely rewarding when it all comes together.

—Jonathan Deans, Sound Co-Designer

The "O" theatre has an extremely complex and powerful sound system, both to deliver the music and sounds of the production to the audience, and for the artists and crew to communicate with each other.

The musicians perform on two stages that are acoustically isolated from the theatre by glass. This set-up protects the instruments from humidity and enhances the sound by allowing the use of studio-quality microphones that eliminate feedback.

The front of house sound-booth is equipped with a Cadac F-type with sixty-four dual inputs, feeding ten Level Control System LD-88s. This provides the ability to automate mixes and dynamic changes, and facilitates movement of sound throughout the room. Seven computers are used to provide cue control, amplifier control, as well as monitoring and acoustical analysis.

A Crest LMX console provides monitor mixes for each of

the ten musicians. The mix stems are fed to each band member's own Yamaha Pro-Mix. For processing, the system uses a Lexicon PCM 80, PCM 90, and two 300s controlled by a LARC.

To enable the cast and crew to hear underwater, the sound department developed the "Neptune System," an underwater microphone/public address system. Vega wireless microphones and Garwood in-ear monitoring are also used to hear cues and music.

The pool was equipped with twelve custom-mounted underwater speakers designed and built by Clark Synthesis of Denver, Colorado. There are two mobile speakers, known as "rovers," used when the aquatic masking is active so the swimmers can still hear cues and music.

An additional Clearcom communications system was installed to interface with the dive-com system in the water. It has twelve channels linking 196 lines at various points in the theatre which can be assigned different matrices.

The Theatre

We created a theatre where people would feel taken away to another era when romance and beauty prevailed, while combining classic architecture with the most advanced and state-of-the-art technology.

—**Patrick Bergé, Scéno Plus**

The concept of staging an aquatic show at Bellagio was conceived in late 1994 by Cirque du Soleil and Mirage Resorts. Groundbreaking for the Bellagio Theatre occurred in February of 1996 and construction was completed in January of 1998.

The interior of the theatre and the stage were conceptualized by Michel Crête and Michel Aubé. The unique 1,800-seat theatre was designed and created by the designers of Cirque du Soleil and Scéno Plus in Montréal and Atlandia Design in Las Vegas over a two-and-a-half-year period. It reflects the style of a fourteenth-century European opera house with tiered balcony seating. The height of the stage from the bottom of the pool to the ceiling is 145 feet—the equivalent of a nine-story building. This is the first time a Cirque du Soleil production has been staged in a proscenium theatre.

The designers wanted to give the theatre a ceiling worthy of the great theatres of the world. With the help of Luc Lafortune, Lighting Designer for Cirque du Soleil, they imagined a dome of metal mesh surrounded by 4,330 MR-16 halogen bulbs, which create a variety of lighting effects. The wire mesh reflects and refracts light, producing dramatic mood changes throughout the production.

In designing the Bellagio Theatre, the creative team faced a major constraint: controlling the temperature and humidity of the environment. The atmosphere had to be sufficiently warm for the performers on stage, and sufficiently cool for the audience at the same time. Engineers therefore employed a ventilation technique to stratify the air in the theatre, thereby creating two different micro-climates. With cold air vents providing air at fifty-five degrees from under each patron's chair, the seating area can be kept at a comfortable seventy-two degrees. The wire mesh dome acts as a chimney allowing the warm air to escape the theatre. The theatre is equipped with thirty-nine video monitors located throughout the backstage area. A twenty-nine-camera closed-circuit MATV system provides twenty-four different views of the show-room, three of which from underwater.

A team of twenty designers participated in the planning process, and more than 400 people worked on the construction of this modern and avant-garde theatre.

The Props

Fifteen original props were designed and built for "O" at the Studio, Cirque du Soleil's International Headquarters in Montréal. These props include giant anemones, four horses, an iceberg, a motorized umbrella raft, a stainless steel piano, a giant marionette, and a floating crocodile mask. Fiberglass is the material most widely used in designing and building these elaborate props.

All set elements were designed to be resistant to corrosion, rust, and humidity. The designers advocated the use of stainless steel for the set pieces and props, a Cirque du Soleil first, even though it is twice as expensive as steel or aluminum and requires the use of more costly welding processes.

The four horses, which make their stunning debut during the unveiling of the Duo Trapèze, are also made of fiberglass. The horses run on battery power, and are equipped with propellers under their tails allowing the horses to glide over the water surface. Inside each horse is a propulsion and flotation module that weighs it down, setting the waterline. The artist riding the horse can steer it with two levers; the clutch system used has three forward speeds and one reverse. Each horse weighs approximately 750 pounds.

The floating crocodile mask, which provides an unusual exit for the Mongolian contortionists, is sculpted from fiberglass-laminated styrofoam. The mask is operated by a technician below the water's surface. It is motor-driven from the rear and can carry up to nine people. "O" is the first Cirque du Soleil production to utilize trolling boat motors in props.

The moveable platform used in the Barge segment is 3,500 pounds of foam and fiberglass. It maneuvers into place with the help of seven divers below the surface and can hold more than twenty performers. The platform is equipped with fourteen breathing stations on its underside for artists who must stay submerged for extended periods of time during the act. The Bateau is another unique Cirque du Soleil creation. This chromally steel apparatus has parallel bars with catch chairs positioned on opposite sides. This is the first time these two disciplines have been combined in one single apparatus.

Three modified Russian Swings, weighing 1,200 pounds each, were constructed of chromally and stainless steel for this production. The swing located in the center of the pool is actually two separate pieces—the swing, which is lowered into position by the carousel, and the base, which is completely submerged under the surface of the water, maneuvered into position, and stored by the divers who then secure the base to the swing.

The Pool

The centerpiece and recurring element in "O" is the massive pool, which holds more than 1.5 million gallons of water and reaches a depth of twenty-five feet. The dimensions of the pool are 150 by 100 feet at the widest point. The water is cycled through a complex filtering system. It takes six hours for all 1.5 million gallons to pass through the system. The pool temperature is kept at eighty-seven degrees.

The pool takes approximately twelve hours to fill and is drained annually for maintenance. When the water is drained it flows into the lake at the front of Bellagio and raises the water level one inch.

Working with water required three years of intensive study and research by the Cirque du Soleil creators. A twenty by thirty foot testing pool was built on the site in October 1997 to examine the water's effects on different materials. At the same time, a mock-up of the floor and gutter around the pool was also built. Three four-inch-thick Plexiglas windows were installed in the pool to test water pressure, lighting colors, and special effects techniques. The lighting department conducted extensive heat testing on the windows. Additional research was also carried out to find a way of eliminating the noise caused by waves of water breaking against the walls of the pool. The gutter around the basin contains different-sized pebbles, which completely absorb the noise as waves hitting the edge are dissipated.

The pool contains seven sophisticated hydraulic lifts that can create a conventional stage surface or reshape the surface of the water. The fifty-three by ninety foot space is unpredictable: a character may be walking on water at one moment, and suddenly be underwater the next, due to lifts that are raised and lowered continuously during the show.

There are four primary scissor lifts and three auxiliary lifts. The four primary lifts can move eighteen and a half feet up and down at speeds ranging from five to twenty feet per minute. Each lift is powered by three hydraulic rams and has a 100,000-pound weight capacity. Additionally, the three auxiliary lifts constructed of steel and fiberglass facilitate stage access for the performers.

The Aquatics

"O" has a team of fourteen divers working every show. Two diving safety officers are outfitted with AGA full-face masks with built-in microphones, which enable them to communicate with stage personnel. The masks are equipped with speakers that actually conduct sound behind the divers' ears through their skulls. The entire cast is scuba-certified and can utilize any one of the eighteen breathing stations underwater. Each diver is outfitted with a personal dive computer to monitor the amount of compressed air used. It has an alarm to indicate if ascent is too rapid and if they have been underwater too long.

The aquatic masking system consists of over one mile (6,000 feet) of hose installed along the bottom of the pool. The hose is perforated to produce air bubbles, which serve to hide underwater activity.

The story begins in 1982, in Baie-Saint-Paul, Québec. In this haven of creativity whose rural charm attracts artists, art collectors, and tourists alike, a group of young street performers mix with the crowd, walking on stilts, juggling, and eating fire. Inspired by the spectators' obvious delight, the performers hatch the idea of organizing an entertainers' festival—the precursor of what is to become Cirque du Soleil.

1984   **Cirque du Soleil** is born with the assistance of the Québec government, as part of the celebrations surrounding the 450th anniversary of Jacques Cartier's arrival in Canada. Cirque is based on a totally new concept: a striking, dramatic mix of circus arts and street entertainment featuring wildly outrageous costumes, staged under magical lighting, and set to original music. With not a single animal in the ring, Cirque's difference is clear from the very start. The show debuts in the small Québec town of Gaspé, and is then performed in ten other cities throughout the province. The first blue-and-yellow big top seats 800.

1985   After performing in Montréal, Sherbrooke, and Québec City, Cirque du Soleil leaves its home province for the first time to take its show to neighboring Ontario. It performs in Ottawa, Toronto, and Niagara Falls.

1986   Cirque du Soleil takes **La Magie Continue** to eight other cities across Canada, including Vancouver, where it puts on several performances at the Children's Festival and Expo 86. Cirque makes its name on the international stage too, as acts are awarded top honors at competitions and festivals around the world. As interest in Cirque grows, so does the big top, which now has room for 1,500 spectators.

1987   Cirque du Soleil visits its American neighbors for the first time. Having triumphed in five cities in Québec, **Le Cirque Réinventé** is performed at the Los Angeles Festival, and then moves on to San Diego and Santa Monica. Exhilarated by the Californian public's response, Cirque du Soleil is an overnight success.

1988   **Le Cirque Réinventé** continues its North American tour, after a brief appearance at the Calgary Winter Olympics. It stops in San Francisco, New York, and Washington, and spends several weeks dazzling Toronto. Wherever it goes, the result is the same: the performances sell out and the critics rave.

1989   Miami, Chicago, and Phoenix are added to the **Le Cirque Réinventé** tour.

1990   Montréal is the setting for the world premiere of a brand-new production, **Nouvelle Expérience**, in a new, 2,500-seat big top. The show then hits the road for an extensive run in California. With this new production, Cirque du Soleil shatters all previous records for ticket sales, and decides to make its first foray into Europe, staging **Le Cirque Réinventé** in London and Paris. The overseas excursions have just begun.

1991   **Nouvelle Expérience** continues on its travels across North America, visiting Atlanta for the first time. By the end of an extensive nineteen-month tour of Canada and the United States, 1.3 million spectators have cheered the show.

1992   Cirque du Soleil crosses the Pacific and makes a name for itself in the Land of the Rising Sun with **Fascination**, a collage of the best acts from past shows. The show opens in Tokyo and then moves on to seven other cities, for a total of 118 performances in four months. Meanwhile, in Europe, Cirque du Soleil joins forces with Switzerland's Circus Knie and stages a show in over sixty towns throughout the country. In North America, 1992 sees Cirque du Soleil make its Las Vegas debut when **Nouvelle Expérience** kicks off a year-long engagement under a big top at the Mirage Hotel. Already juggling several productions, Cirque du Soleil adds a monument to its repertoire of shows: **Saltimbanco**. Premiering in Montréal, this latest production begins a lengthy tour of North America.

1993   Following **Nouvelle Expérience**'s successful run in Las Vegas, Cirque du Soleil moves into a theatre built to its specifications at the new Treasure Island Hotel. A ten-year contract is signed with Mirage Resorts to stage **Mystère**, a gigantic production befitting this show business capital. **Saltimbanco** completes its nineteen-month North American tour of a dozen cities, receiving resounding ovations from 1.4 million spectators.

1994	*Saltimbanco* embarks on a six-month run in Tokyo in 1994 that attracts a great deal of attention. The same year, Cirque du Soleil celebrates its tenth anniversary with another production, **Alegría**. True to tradition, the two-year North American tour is launched in Montréal. Meanwhile, **Mystère** continues to create a sensation in Las Vegas, and **Saltimbanco** returns to Montréal for a brief run.
1995	While **Alegría** pursues its triumphant North American tour, Cirque du Soleil responds to a request from the Canadian government and creates a show for the heads of state gathered at the G7 Summit in Halifax, Nova Scotia. Also in 1995, **Saltimbanco** sets out to conquer Europe. Cirque's spectacular white big top with seating for 2,500 spectators makes its first stop in Amsterdam, followed by Munich, Berlin, Düsseldorf, and Vienna. Amsterdam becomes the site of Cirque du Soleil's European Headquarters.
1996	In April, Cirque launches **Quidam** in Montréal. After finishing its hometown run, **Quidam** heads off on a three-year North American tour. Meanwhile, **Saltimbanco** continues its European tour, with stops in London, Hamburg, Stuttgart, Antwerp, Zurich and Frankfurt, while **Alegría** sets out to tour Asia for a few months.
1997	**Quidam** continues to capture the hearts of North American spectators, adding two new cities, Denver and Houston, to the tour. On the other side of the Atlantic, the curtain falls on **Saltimbanco** at London's Royal Albert Hall, marking the end of a two-year European tour. **Alegría** kicks off its own tour of Europe a few weeks later. But Cirque du Soleil's adventures do not end there. The year 1997 begins with the inauguration of the brand new International Headquarters in Montréal, the Studio, where all of Cirque's shows will be created and produced.
1998	While **Alegría** pursues its journey across Europe, **Quidam** finishes up its North American tour, which includes a stopover in Dallas, a first for Cirque du Soleil. During its three-year tour, almost 1,000 performances have been held under the blue-and-yellow big top. All in all, over 2,500,000 North American spectators have applauded **Quidam**. Furthermore, in October 1998, Cirque du Soleil's second resident show, "O," takes to the stage of a new theatre at the Bellagio in Las Vegas. This production is Cirque's first aquatic show. In December of the same year, Cirque inaugurates yet another permanent show, *La Nouba*, at the Walt Disney World Resort near Orlando, Florida. Cirque du Soleil also restages **Saltimbanco** in Ottawa for a few weeks before sending it off on an Asia-Pacific tour scheduled to last three years.
1999	**Saltimbanco** sets up shop in Asia and the Pacific and begins a three-year tour of the region in Sydney. In March, **Quidam** embarks on a four-year European tour in Amsterdam. In addition, Cirque du Soleil's brand-new production, **Dralion**, launches its North American tour in Montréal. **Alegría** finds a permanent home at Beau Rivage, a new resort in Biloxi, Mississippi, and the dinner show **Pomp Duck and Circumstance** sets off on a European tour. To top it all off, the multimedia division, Cirque du Soleil Images, releases its first feature film, "Alegria," inspired by the show of the same name. Its dynamic team also produces "**Cirque du Soleil Presents Quidam**," a spectacular television version of the show to be aired around the globe.
2000	Audiences on three continents continue to marvel at Cirque du Soleil's four resident shows (**La Nouba**, **Mystère**, "O," and **Alegría**) and three touring productions (**Quidam**, **Saltimbanco** and **Dralion**). In the year 2000 alone, close to six million spectators attend Cirque du Soleil shows worldwide. Moreover, movie fans enjoy seeing Cirque du Soleil in its first-ever large-format IMAX production, entitled "**Journey of Man**" ("**Passages**" in French).

The international success story known as Cirque du Soleil is above all the story of a remarkable bond between performers and spectators the world over. At the end of the day, it is the spectators who spark the creative passions of Cirque du Soleil.

O: Cirque du Soleil at Bellagio

Published in the United States by powerHouse Books,
a division of powerHouse Cultural Entertainment, Inc.
180 Varick Street, Suite 1302, New York, NY 10014-4606
telephone 212 604 9074, fax 212 366 5247
e-mail: cirque@powerHouseBooks.com
website: www.powerHouseBooks.com

First edition, 2001

Library of Congress Cataloging-in-Publication Data:

Vial, Véronique.
    O : Cirque du Soleil at the Bellagio / Photographs by Véronique Vial.
    p. cm.
  ISBN 1-57687-094-4
    1. Stage photography--Nevada--Las Vegas. 2. Cirque du Soleil--Pictorial works. 3.
Circus--Nevada--Las Vegas--Pictorial works. I. Title.

TR817 .V53 2000
791.3'09714--dc21

                                                                    00-058462

Hardcover ISBN 1-57687-094-4

Separations, printing, and binding by Artegrafica, Verona

A complete catalog of powerHouse Books and Limited Editions
is available upon request; please call, write, or swim to our website.

10 9 8 7 6 5 4 3 2 1

Printed and bound in Italy

art Direction: robert Avellan_r+ave/la